© 2002 by Barbour Publishing, Inc.

ISBN 1-58660-438-4

Cover art © Photodisc, Inc.

Published by Barbour Books, an imprint of Barbour Publishing, Inc.
P.O. Box 719, Uhrichsville, Ohio 44683
www.barbourbooks.com

Member of the
Evangelical Christian
Publishers Association

Printed in China.

A Heartfelt Thanks

REBECCA GERMANY

From the depths of my heart to yours.

"Priceless little memories
are treasures without price,
And through the gateway of the heart
they lead to paradise."

WILLIAM WORDSWORTH

How can I truly say thanks for all you have done for me?

"I thank my God every time I remember you."

PHILIPPIANS 1:3

A Story of Thanks

There was a small ant who had a big goal to carry a huge, mouth-watering corn chip back to the ant hill. Along the way, his load shifted, fell, and wedged between two rocks.

The ant exercised all his own strength of body and mind to move the prized load, but it did not budge.

So, he prayed. . .and prayed hard.

God sent a gentle breeze to rock the corn chip. Still, it remained pinned between its captors.

God sent a light rain to wiggle the corn chip out of the firm grasp. And yet, it had no affect.

Finally, God sent another ant along the path. Teaming together, the ants were able to move the corn chip out of the rocky vise and home.

God knows how much we need the help and support of others. Since you allowed God to use you, it is as if I feel His touch through you.

I thank Him for sending you along my path.

"*We* all of us need assistance.
Those who sustain others themselves want to be sustained."

MAURICE HULST
The Way of the Heart

"Feeling gratitude and not expressing it
is like wrapping a present and not giving it."

WILLIAM ARTHUR WARD

*"They may forget what you said,
but they will never forget
how you made them feel."*

CARL W. BUECHNER

*"Always giving thanks to
God the Father for everything,
in the name of our Lord Jesus Christ."*

EPHESIANS 5:20

"When home is ruled according to God's Word,
angels might be asked to stay with us,
and they would not find themselves out of their element."

CHARLES H. SPURGEON

"For sunlit hours and visions clear,
For all remembered faces dear,
For comrades of a single day,
Who sent us stronger on our way,
For friends who shared the year's long road,
And bore with us the common load,
For hours that levied heavy tolls,
But brought us nearer to our goals,
For insights won through toil and tears,
We thank the Keeper of our years."

CLYDE McGEE

*Know that though
I may not say
thanks often enough
or loud enough,
God sees what you do
to His glory.*

"The sweetest of all sounds is praise."

XENOPHON,
Athenian philosopher

From me:

> "I have not stopped giving thanks for you,
> remembering you in my prayers."

EPHESIANS 1:16

From God:

> *"I know your deeds,*
> *your hard work and your perseverance."*

REVELATION 2:2

"*Then* the King will say to those on his right, 'Come, you who are blessed by my Father; take your inheritance, the kingdom prepared for you since the creation of the world. For I was hungry and you gave me something to eat, I was thirsty and you gave me something to drink, I was a stranger and you invited me in, I needed clothes and you clothed me, I was sick and you looked after me, I was in prison and you came to visit me.'

"Then the righteous will answer him, 'Lord, when did we see you hungry and feed you, or thirsty and give you something to drink? When did we see you a stranger and invite you in, or needing clothes and clothe you? When did we see you sick or in prison and go to visit you?'

"The King will reply, 'I tell you the truth, whatever you did for one of the least of these brothers of mine, you did for me.'"

MATTHEW 25:34–40

No Matter
Great or small —
you have touched my life.

Great

"*Be* not afraid of greatness:
some are born great, some achieve greatness,
and some have greatness thrust upon them."

WILLIAM SHAKESPEARE

"*Greatness lies, not in being strong,
but in the right use of strength.*"

HENRY WARD BEECHER

*"No one is so generous as
he who has nothing to give."*

FRENCH PROVERB

"Generosity is not giving me that which
I need more than you do,
but it is giving me that which
you need more than I do."

KAHLIL GIBRAN
Sand and Foam

Small

"There are no great things,
only small things with great love. Happy are those."

MOTHER TERESA

"The best portion of a good man's life,
his little, nameless, unremembered acts
of kindness and of love."

WILLIAM WORDSWORTH

"*I* long to accomplish a great and noble task,
but it is my chief duty to accomplish humble tasks
as though they were great and noble."

HELEN KELLER

"*A* cheerful look brings joy to the heart,
and good news gives health to the bones."

PROVERBS 15:30

"*How* lovely to think that no one need wait a moment, we can start now, start slowly changing the world! How lovely that everyone, great and small, can make their contribution toward introducing justice straightaway. . . And you can always, always give something, even if it is only kindness!"

ANNE FRANK

Though you may never know the extent of the touch you have made on my life, you are a blessing to me.

*"Anyone who does what is good
is from God."*

3 John 11

"When we do the best that we can,
we never know what miracle is wrought
in our life, or in the life of another."

Helen Keller

"*You* will be made rich in every way
so that you can be generous on every occasion,
and through us your generosity will
result in thanksgiving to God."

2 CORINTHIANS 9:11

"*The return we reap from generous actions
is not always evident.*"

FRANCESCO GUICCIARDINI
Counsels and Reflections

"*Every* soul that touches yours—
Be it the slightest contact—
Gets therefrom some good;
Some little grace; one kindly thought;
One aspiration yet unfelt;
One bit of courage
For the darkening sky;
One gleam of faith
To brave the thickening ills of life;
One glimpse of brighter skies—
To make this life worthwhile
And heaven a surer heritage."

GEORGE ELIOT

"You get the best out of others when you give the best of yourself."

HARRY FIRESTONE

"If you treat a person as he is, he will stay as he is;
but if you treat him as if he were
what he ought to be and could be,
he will become what he ought to be and could be."

JOHANN WOLFGANG VON GOETHE

"I have met people so empty of joy that when I clasped their frosty fingertips it seemed as if I were shaking hands with a northeast storm. Others there are whose hands have sunbeams in them, so that their grasp warms my heart. It may be only the clinging touch of a child's hand, but there is as much potential sunshine in it for me as there is in a loving glance for others."

HELEN KELLER

"Those who bring sunshine to the lives of others cannot keep it from themselves."

JAMES BARRIE

"Laughter is the shortest distance between two people."

VICTOR BORGE

"*Every* experience God gives us,
every person He puts in our lives,
is the perfect preparation for
the future that only He can see."

CORRIE TEN BOOM

"*The true meaning of life is to plant trees,
under whose shade you do not expect to sit.*"

NELSON HENDERSON

"*He* who has done his best for his own time
has lived for all times."

JOHANN VON SCHILLER

I will never forget.

"*Never* shall I forget the days
which I spent with you."

LUDWIG VAN BEETHOVEN

Stitched in Time

Knowing you has added another square to the quilt of my life. The fabric is stamped with your unique touch. The pieces are woven with the memories of our time together. The stitching is firm, binding our friendship for eternity.

"Some people weave burlap into the fabric of our lives,
and some weave gold thread.
Both contribute to make the whole picture
beautiful and unique."

AUTHOR UNKNOWN

*Because of you,
I can be a blessing too.*

Gratitude cannot truly be repaid unless it is passed along in acts of kindness to someone else.

"If you can't return a favor, pass it on."

LOUISE BROWN

Because your heart was aglow with kindness toward me, my heart now glows.

"Goodness is uneventful, it does not flash, it glows."

DAVID GRAYSON

"The best way to cheer yourself up is to try to cheer somebody else up."

MARK TWAIN

I am inspired to carry kindness to others.

"*As* we express our gratitude,
we must never forget that the highest appreciation
is not to utter words,
but to live by them."

JOHN FITZGERALD KENNEDY

Soon a simple kindness started with one can reach out to a multitude.

"*The* best way to keep good acts in memory
is to repeat them."

CATO

"*The greatest use of life is to spend it for
something that will outlast it.*"

WILLIAM JAMES

The cycle of kindness continues, snowballing along the way.

"Remember this:
Whoever sows sparingly will also reap sparingly,
and whoever sows generously will also reap generously."

2 CORINTHIANS 9:6

*"Don't judge each day by the harvest you reap
but by the seeds that you plant."*

ROBERT LOUIS STEVENSON

So, give and you will receive.

"*The joy that you give to others is
the joy that comes back to you.*"

JOHN GREENLEAF WHITTIER

"*It* is one of the most beautiful compensations of life,
that no man can sincerely try to help another
without helping himself."

RALPH WALDO EMERSON

"*Do* all the good you can, by all the means you can, in all the ways you can, in all the places you can, at all the times you can, to all the people you can, as long as ever you can."

JOHN WESLEY

"*When* your burden is heaviest, you can always lighten a little some other burden. At the times when you cannot see God, there is still open to you this sacred possibility, to show God; for it is the love and kindness of human hearts through which the divine reality come home to men, whether they name it or not. Let this thought, then, stay with you: there may be times when you cannot find help, but there is no time when you cannot give help."

GEORGE S. MERRIAM

My heart rejoices in knowing you.

"*Dear* friend,
I pray that you may enjoy good health
and that all may go well with you,
even as your soul is getting along well."

3 JOHN 2

Thanks for all you mean to me.